THE ULTIMATE
KANSAS CITY CHIEFS
TRIVIA BOOK

A Collection of Amazing Trivia Quizzes
and Fun Facts for Die-Hard Chiefs Fans!

Ray Walker

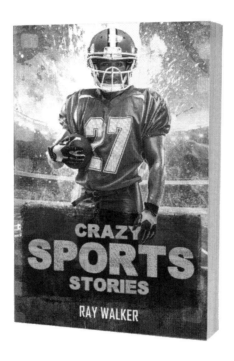

CONTENTS

INTRODUCTION

Team fandom should be inspirational. Our attachment to our favorite teams should fill us with pride, excitement, loyalty, and a sense of fulfillment in knowing that we are part of a community with many other fans who feel the same way.

Chiefs' fans are no exception. With a rich, successful history in the NFL, the Kansas City Chiefs have inspired their supporters to strive for greatness with their tradition of colorful players, memorable eras, big moves, and unique moments.

This book is meant to be a celebration of those moments and an examination of the collection of interesting, impressive, or important details that allow us to understand the full stories behind the players and the team.

You may use the book as you wish. Each chapter contains 20 quiz questions in a mixture of multiple-choice and true-or-false formats, an answer key (don't worry, it's on a separate page!), and a section of 10 "Did You Know" facts about the team.

Some will use it to test themselves with the quiz questions. How much Chiefs history do you really know? How many of the finer points can you remember?

Some will use it competitively, because isn't that the heart of sports, waging contests with friends and fellow devotees to see who can lay claim to being the biggest fan? Some will enjoy it as a learning experience, gaining insight to enrich their fandom and add color to their understanding of their favorite team. Still others may use it to teach, sharing the wonderful anecdotes inside to inspire a new generation of fans to hop aboard the Chiefs bandwagon.

Whatever your purpose may be, we hope you enjoy delving into the amazing background of Kansas City Chiefs football!

Oh, for the record, information and statistics in this book are current up to the beginning of 2021. The Chiefs will surely topple more records and win more awards as the seasons pass, so keep this in mind when you're watching the next game with your friends, and someone starts a conversation with "Did you know…."

CHAPTER 1:

ORIGINS & HISTORY

QUIZ TIME!

1. In which year did the franchise begin playing in the American Football League?

    a. 1949

    b. 1957

    c. 1960

    d. 1966

2. The franchise was nearly called the Kansas City Blues, partly to reference the style of southern music made popular in the area and partly to honor a defunct rugby team from the city by that name.

    a. True

    b. False

3. How was the nickname "Chiefs" chosen for the team?

    a. As a homage to Chief Sitting Bull, whose tribe had long occupied land in the area.

    b. The founder also owned a petroleum company called

Big Chief Oil and wanted a name that tied in with this business.

c. It was selected as an American version of the leadership theme that ran through Kansas City's other teams, such as the Monarchs and Royals.

d. It came from a fan's suggestion in a contest that referred to the nickname of Kansas City's mayor at the time.

4. In which season did the Chiefs begin to play in their new stadium, Arrowhead Stadium, after moving from their former home at Municipal Stadium?

   a. 1963
   b. 1969
   c. 1972
   d. 1980

5. Who was the founder of the Kansas City Chiefs?

   a. Lamar Hunt
   b. b. Hank Stram
   c. c. Art Rooney
   d. d. Tom Landry

6. In which season did the Chiefs earn their first playoff berth?

   a. 1960
   b. 1962
   c. 1986
   d. 1990

7. The Kansas City Chiefs won more games than any other NFL team during the period between 1990 and 2000.

    a. True
    b. False

8. How many times have the Chiefs won a division title?

    a. 5 times
    b. 8 times
    c. 10 times
    d. 13 times

9. Which of the following players was NOT among the first Chiefs ever to be named as Kansas City's representatives for the All-Pro Team in 1960?

    a. Quarterback Len Dawson
    b. Linebacker Sherrill Headrick
    c. Tight end Fred Arbanas
    d. Halfback Abner Hayes

10. Where do the Kansas City Chiefs rank among NFL franchises in Super Bowl Championship trophies won?

    a. Fourth overall
    b. Tied for 9th overall
    c. Tied for 16th overall
    d. 22nd overall

11. How did the Chiefs fare during their 50th anniversary season in the NFL?

    a. Failed to make the playoffs
    b. Lost in the first round to the New England Patriots

c. Lost in the conference finals to the Indianapolis Colts

d. Won the Super Bowl over the San Francisco 49ers

12. The longest stretch the Chiefs have gone without making the playoffs is 14 years, from 1972 through 1985.

   a. True

   b. False

13. Which team did Kansas City face in its first NFL game after the AFL-NFL merger, which resulted in a 27-10 loss?

   a. Baltimore Colts

   b. St. Louis Cardinals

   c. Denver Broncos

   d. Minnesota Vikings

14. What were the details surrounding the Chiefs' first shutout in the NFL?

   a. 1970, a 28-0 loss to the San Diego Chargers on the road

   b. 1970, a 16-0 victory over the Denver Broncos at home

   c. 1971, a 9-0 victory over the Dallas Cowboys on the road

   d. 1973, a 14-0 loss to the Buffalo Bills at home

15. Which player kicked the first field goal for the franchise?

   a. Harrison Butker

   b. Jan Stenerud

   c. Jack Spikes

   d. Tommy Brooker

16. Kansas City is tied with the Green Bay Packers and Chicago Bears as the franchises that have sent more players to the Pro Bowl than any other NFL franchise.

    a. True
    b. False

17. How did Kansas City fare in its first NFL playoff run?

    a. Won the Super Bowl over the Chicago Bears
    b. Lost in the divisional playoffs to the Miami Dolphins
    c. Lost in the conference finals to the Baltimore Colts
    d. Lost in the Super Bowl to the New York Giants

18. What is the franchise record for most victories in a single regular season?

    a. 11 wins
    b. 12 wins
    c. 13 wins
    d. 14 wins

19. The Chiefs have had two mascots, one a human in a costume and the other a real horse. What are the names of these Kansas City mascots?

    a. Scout and Tomahawk
    b. Casey Cougar and Geronimo
    c. K.C. Wolf and Warpaint
    d. Running Bear and Fleetfoot

20. The Kansas City football franchise has, at some point, been in both the Western Conference and the Eastern Conference.

a. True
b. False

QUIZ ANSWERS

1. C – 1960

2. B – False

3. D – It came from a fan's suggestion in a contest that referred to the nickname of Kansas City's mayor at the time.

4. C – 1972

5. A – Lamar Hunt

6. B – 1962

7. B – False

8. D – 13 times

9. C – Tight end Fred Arbanas

10. C – Tied for 16th overall

11. A – Failed to make the playoffs

12. A – True

13. D – Minnesota Vikings

14. B – 1970, in a 16 – 0 victory over the Denver Broncos at home

15. C – Jack Spikes

16. B – False

17. B – Lost in the divisional playoffs to the Miami Dolphins

18. D – 14 wins

19. C – K.C. Wolf and Warpaint

20. B – False

DID YOU KNOW?

1. Nearly everything about the franchise is different today from its beginning. In 1960, when the team was founded, it was part of the American Football League, a rival of the NFL. It was located in Dallas, Texas, rather than Kansas City, Missouri, and the team was known as the Texans, not the Chiefs.

2. The franchise moved to Kansas City in 1963 and changed its nickname to the Chiefs at the same time. Joining the NFL did not come until 1970 when the AFL and NFL merged.

3. At the outset, the team played at the Cotton Bowl in Dallas, Texas, and shared the field with the Dallas Cowboys for three seasons. Since 1972, Arrowhead Stadium has been their home, giving the Chiefs the sixth largest stadium in the NFL, with a seating capacity of 76,416 people.

4. While the Chiefs are the anchor tenant of Arrowhead Stadium, they share a parking area and complex with Major League Baseball's Kansas City Royals. When this situation developed in the 1970s, it was the first time in North America that a complex was created for two big-league franchises in different sports.

5. As a new team entering the AFL in 1960, the Chiefs paid a $25,000 franchise fee for the right to join the league. In contrast, the Dallas Cowboys, who joined the NFL that

same year, paid $1 million. And, for current context, when the Houston Texans joined in 2002, they paid an expansion fee of $700 million.

6. The first touchdown in franchise history was scored when the team was still located in Dallas and known as the Texans. On September 10, 1960, Chris Burford caught a pass from Cotton Davidson for a 12-yard score.

7. Kansas City's biggest NFL rival is generally thought to be the Las Vegas Raiders because the two teams have long been in the same division and have played more than twice as many games as any of Kansas City's other non-division opponents. The Chiefs have the advantage in the head-to-head rivalry, 68-54-2, but the Raiders have won more Super Bowl championships, 3-2.

8. Kansas City's franchise record for fewest victories recorded by the club in a single regular season is just 2, which they set during the 1977 season and later matched in 2008 and 2012.

9. For over four decades, the TD Pack Band performed every time the Chiefs played at home. Band founder Tony DiPardo wrote songs for the team such as the "Hank Stram Polka" and the "Chiefs are on the Warpath." DiPardo was even given a Chiefs Super Bowl ring after Kansas City's victory in 1970.

10. In the beginning, the Dallas Texans were competitive in the AFL. They finished second in 1960 and 1961, before breaking through with a first-place finish and a league

championship in their final season before moving to Kansas City.

CHAPTER 2:

JERSEYS & NUMBERS

QUIZ TIME!

1. When they began playing in the AFL in 1960 as the Dallas Texans, the team used what color scheme for their home and away uniforms?

   a. Blue and orange
   b. Red, white, and blue
   c. Green and white
   d. Red and gold

2. The numbers 0 and 00 have been banned from circulation by Kansas City's ownership because they are seen to represent a losing attitude.

   a. True
   b. False

3. How many stripes are on the sleeves of the current version of the red Chiefs jersey?

   a. One yellow stripe
   b. One white stripe and one yellow stripe

c. Two white stripes and one yellow stripe

d. Two yellow stripes

4. The Kansas City Chiefs have retired three numbers for each of two different position groups, while no other position group has more than one number retired. Which two have the Chiefs honored most?

a. Running back and linebacker

b. Quarterback and defensive line

c. Wide receiver and defensive back

d. Tight end and offensive line

5. In which year was approval received for player names to appear on the backs of Chiefs jerseys?

a. 1963

b. 1970

c. 1984

d. 1989

6. Which jersey number has sold the most Kansas City jerseys on NFL.com?

a. Wide receiver Tyreek Hill's No. 10

b. Tight end Travis Kelce's No. 87

c. Running back Clyde Edwards-Helaire's No. 25

d. Quarterback Patrick Mahomes' No. 15

7. The white jerseys worn by Kansas City are often said to have been "jinxed" and therefore the team avoids wearing them during the Super Bowl whenever the choice is theirs.

a. True

b. False

8. Who is the player who wore the lowest-numbered retired jersey in Chiefs franchise history?

    a. Quarterback Len Dawson
    b. Cornerback Emmitt Thomas
    c. Kicker Jan Stenerud
    d. Linebacker Willie Lanier

9. The current version of the Chiefs uniform includes three colors. Which of the following is NOT included in the color scheme?

    a. Red
    b. Black
    c. White
    d. Gold

10. Only two numbers have been worn by a single player in Kansas City Chiefs franchise history. Which numbers are these?

    a. No. 4 and No. 37
    b. No. 9 and No. 83
    c. No. 16 and No. 28
    d. No. 62 and No. 94

11. Twenty players have worn No. 87 for the Chiefs. Which of these players scored the most career touchdowns?

    a. Wide receiver Eddie Kennison
    b. Tight end Walt Arnold
    c. Wide receiver Tamarick Vanover
    d. Tight end Travis Kelce

12. The Chiefs have worn throwback uniforms from time to time but have never in their history sported an alternate jersey.

    a. True
    b. False

13. Why did running back Darwin Thompson choose to wear No. 25 on his jersey for Kansas City?

    a. To symbolize his weekly goal: 25 rushing yards per quarter, resulting in a 100-yard game
    b. To represent his draft position, as he was taken 25th overall by Kansas City
    c. To honor former Chiefs running back Jamaal Charles, whom he asked for permission to wear the number
    d. To reference the month and day of his birth date, February 5

14. How many jersey numbers have the Kansas City Chiefs retired for their former players?

    a. 7 numbers
    b. 10 numbers
    c. 12 numbers
    d. 15 numbers

15. Which player competed for the Chiefs for just one preseason and played no regular season or playoff games with the club; the shortest tenure of anyone whose number has been retired by the franchise?

    a. Cornerback Emmitt Thomas
    b. Running back Stone Johnson

c.   Running back Abner Haynes

d.   Running back Mack Lee Hill

16. Eight players have worn the No. 1 for Kansas City and every single one of them was a quarterback.

a.   True

b.   False

17. Lucky No. 7 has been worn by nine Chiefs players over the years. Which athlete wore it for the most games?

a.   Quarterback Ron Jaworski

b.   Quarterback John Huarte

c.   Kicker Harrison Butker

d.   Quarterback Matt Cassel

18. What Chiefs player most recently had his number retired by the club?

a.   Linebacker Derrick Thomas

b.   Cornerback Emmitt Thomas

c.   Linebacker Willie Lanier

d.   Tight end Tony Gonzalez

19. Which number did star running back Priest Holmes, who was named an All-Pro three times, wear for Kansas City?

a.   No. 11

b.   No. 21

c.   No. 30

d.   No. 31

20. The Chiefs have retired more jersey numbers than any other NFL franchise has.

   a. True
   b. False

QUIZ ANSWERS

1. D – Red and gold

2. B – False

3. C – Two white stripes and one yellow stripe

4. A – Running back and linebacker

5. B – 1970

6. D – Quarterback Patrick Mahomes' No. 15

7. B – False

8. C – Kicker Jan Stenerud

9. B – Black

10. C – No. 16 and No. 28

11. D – Tight end Travis Kelce

12. A – True

13. C – To honor former Chiefs running back Jamaal Charles, whom he asked for permission to wear the number

14. B – 10 numbers

15. B – Running back Stone Johnson

16. B – False

17. C – Kicker Harrison Butker

18. A – Linebacker Derrick Thomas

19. D – No. 31

20. B – False

DID YOU KNOW?

1. Although team founder Lamar Hunt initially wanted to use Columbia Blue as the franchise's main color, Houston Oilers owner Bud Adams grabbed the rights to the color first upon the founding of the AFL, leaving Hunt to go with his second choice instead and creating the color scheme Chiefs fans know today.

2. The highest number ever sported by a Chief is 99. Seventeen players have donned this number, ranging from defensive end Mike Bell, who wore it for 12 seasons between 1979 and 1991, to seven players who used it only for a single year.

3. Franchise superstar quarterback Patrick Mahomes wore No. 5 throughout his high school and college careers but the number was already taken by kicker Cairo Santos when Mahomes joined the Chiefs. Rather than ask Santos to change it or offer compensation, the humble Mahomes, who would later sign the largest contract in NFL history, allowed Santos to keep the number and chose 15 for himself.

4. 2013 marked the first season that Kansas City wore red on red. Against the Dallas Cowboys, the team sported both red pants and a red jersey. While this type of combination is often ridiculed among NFL teams, Kansas City's version

was very popular with fans and is still worn frequently by the squad.

5. After team founder Lamar Hunt passed away in 2007, the Chiefs wore a patch with Hunt's initials on their jerseys for the season. The following year, Kansas City wore the patch again. As of 2021, they have still not removed it, so it is fairly safe to say that the patch is permanent.

6. The Chiefs' helmet logo had to be changed when the team moved from Dallas to Kansas City because the state of Texas would no longer be appropriate. Inspiration was taken from the San Francisco 49ers' "SF" lettering and the interlocking "KC" was inserted into an arrowhead shape rather than a regular oval, creating the team's classic look.

7. Superstition may have scared some Chiefs away from wearing the No. 13. Only six players in franchise history have chosen it for themselves and only wide receiver De'Anthony Thomas held onto the number for more than three seasons.

8. Since 1973, the NFL no longer allows players to wear jersey No. 0 or 00. No Kansas City Chief ever wore either number in the 13 seasons before this change, so neither number will be used in franchise history.

9. The highest number ever retired by the Kansas City Chiefs is No. 86, belonging to defensive player Buck Buchanan. Buchanan helped lead the Chiefs to their first Super Bowl victory.

10. Prior to the team's appearance in the Super Bowl in 1970, the Chiefs' equipment manager, Bobby Yarborough, was told to give Kansas City's helmets a fresh coat of paint for the big game. However, players rebelled and demanded that the "seasoned" versions, with chips and scratches, be left intact.

CHAPTER 3:

CATCHY NICKNAMES

QUIZ TIME!

1. By which common nickname is a popular Chiefs fan gesture and chant most commonly referred to?

    a. "The War Cry"

    b. "The Archer's Deluxe"

    c. "The Floating Feather"

    d. "The Tomahawk Chop"

2. Speedy Chiefs wide receiver Tyreek Hill was often referred to as "Junior Bolt" thanks to his 5'10" height and his reverence for Jamaican Olympic sprinter and world record holder Usain Bolt.

    a. True

    b. False

3. Which Chiefs player earned the nickname the "Nigerian Nightmare" because of his heritage and powerful playing style?

    a. Running back Christian Okoye

    b. Linebacker Derrick Thomas

c. Defensive end Tamba Hali

d. Running back Jamaal Charles

4. Which Kansas City player is affectionately known by players and fans as "Hungry Pig"?

a. Defensive tackle Dontari Poe

b. Offensive tackle Jim Tyrer

c. Center Tim Grunhard

d. Linebacker Willie Lanier

5. Why was quarterback Len Dawson known by his teammates as "Lenny the Cool"?

a. Because Dawson always arrived at games wearing a black leather bomber jacket, despite the Kansas City heat

b. Because when asking a question, Dawson ended most of his sentences with "Cool"

c. Because Dawson showed no signs of duress under pressure and remained level-headed

d. Because Dawson insisted that the air conditioning be set at 65 degrees for all team meetings

6. When watching a Chiefs game on television, it is almost inevitable that broadcasters will refer to Kansas City safety Tyrann Mathieu by which moniker that Mathieu has had since his college days?

a. "Smash & Grab"

b. "Tyrann Island"

c. "Stickum"

d. "The Honey Badger"

7. Kansas City tight end Tony Gonzalez was known as "Gonzo" for three reasons: his last name, his love for author Hunter S. Thompson, and his large nose which resembled the Muppet Gonzo's beak.

   a. True
   b. False

8. Why was Kansas City offensive tackle Mitchell Schwartz given the nickname "Bigfoot" by teammates?

   a. Whenever it came time to pick up a dinner check, he was nowhere to be seen.
   b. He has an enormous amount of body hair, which teammates poked fun at in the locker room.
   c. He wears size 18 shoes, which are very hard to shop for.
   d. He accidentally tripped star quarterback Patrick Mahomes while pass blocking, causing Mahomes to miss the next two practices.

9. What is Kansas City head coach Andy Reid also known as?

   a. "Cheeseburger"
   b. "P.P.K." (short for "Punt, Pass, Kick")
   c. "The Commandant"
   d. "Big Red"

10. Chiefs wide receiver Tyreek Hill, who was thought to be the fastest player in the league, went by which one-word nickname?

a. "Flash"

b. "Turbo"

c. "Lightning"

d. "Cheetah"

11. Which Chiefs player was known to fans and teammates by the nicknames the "Human Joystick" for his speed and agility, and the "X Factor" for his celebrations?

    a. Kick returner Dante Hall

    b. Wide receiver Eddie Kennison

    c. Wide receiver Derrick Alexander

    d. Running back Kareem Hunt

12. After having two memorable fights with his former Kansas City teammates as a newly signed member of the Denver Broncos, ex-Chief defensive end Neil Smith earned the nickname the "Vengeful Ex."

    a. True

    b. False

13. Which current Chief is known to teammates by the nickname "Buttkicker"?

    a. Offensive lineman Laurent Duvernay-Tardif

    b. Linebacker Anthony Hitchens

    c. Kicker Harrison Butker

    d. Defensive end Frank Clark

14. An NFL rule informally known as the "Neil Smith Rule," named after the longtime Kansas City defensive lineman, prohibits a defensive player from taking which of the following actions?

a. Flinching in order to cause a false start penalty on the offense
b. Diving into a blocker's ankles from the side or behind
c. Grabbing an opposing player's hair as part of the tackling process
d. Holding the quarterback up to allow help to arrive and push him further backward

15. At times during his tenure in Kansas City, Chiefs Hall-of-Fame quarterback Joe Montana was referred to by all of the following nicknames except for which one?

a. "Joe Cool"
b. "Bird Legs"
c. "The Comeback Kid"
d. "Joey Amazing"

16. Kansas City quarterback Alex Smith was called the "Role Model" by his young teammates because he was brought in to provide leadership and playoff experience while demonstrating how to act like a professional athlete.

a. True
b. False

17. During the 2010s, Kansas City's defense was known for its tendency to penetrate the line of scrimmage and haul down opposing quarterbacks, leading to which of the following nicknames?

a. "The K.C. Sack Attack"
b. "Sacks 5th Avenue"

c. "Sack Nation"

d. "The Pressure"

18. Which famous sportscaster memorably dubbed star Kansas City wide receiver Andre "Bad Moon" Rison?

    a. ESPN's Chris Berman

    b. NBC's Al Michaels

    c. ABC's Bob Costas

    d. Fox's Troy Aikman

19. For eight seasons in Kansas City, wide receiver Dwayne Bowe was referred to as which of the following?

    a. "Dwayne Drops"

    b. "Bowe at Arrowhead"

    c. "Deebo"

    d. "The Bowe Show"

20. Flashy Chiefs running back Charcandrick West was known as "Charknado" because he had a 3000-gallon aquarium installed in his mansion, in which he kept a pet shark.

    a. True

    b. False

QUIZ ANSWERS

1. D – the "Tomahawk Chop"

2. B – False

3. A – Running back Christian Okoye

4. A – Defensive tackle Dontari Poe

5. C – Because Dawson showed no signs of duress under pressure and remained level-headed

6. D – The "Honey Badger"

7. B – False

8. C – He wears size 18 shoes, which are very hard to shop for

9. D – "Big Red"

10. D – "Cheetah"

11. A – Kick returner Dante Hall

12. B – False

13. C – Kicker Harrison Butker

14. A – Flinching in order to cause a false start penalty on the offense

15. D – "Joey Amazing"

16. B – False

17. C – "Sack Nation"

18. A – ESPN's Chris Berman

19. D – The "Bowe Show"

20. B – False

DID YOU KNOW?

1. Kansas City mayor Harold Roe Bartle inspired the nickname "Chiefs." Kansas City beat out other cities who wanted a professional football franchise, in part due to the help of Bartle. To acknowledge his contributions, the team chose to use part of Bartle's nickname as a leader of a Boy Scouts troop, "Chief Lone Bear."

2. The conservative style of football employed by Chiefs coach Marty Schottenheimer was derided by critics as "Marty Ball." This philosophy usually involved a powerful run game, short, safe passes, and a stout defense, but it was not very exciting to watch.

3. Before 1991, the University of Massachusetts used the nickname "Chiefs," which means that when Kansas City selected defensive back Paul Metallo from the school in 1973, his team nickname did not change upon joining the NFL. UMass has since become the "River Hawks," so this phenomenon will not happen again.

4. The up-tempo, high-scoring Chiefs' offense led by quarterback Patrick Mahomes, throwing to tight end Travis Kelce and wide receivers Sammy Watkins, Mecole Hardman, Tyreek Hill, and Demarcus Robinson, was christened the "Legion of Zoom."

5. Fans of Kansas City are often collectively referred to as "Chiefs Kingdom." When they gather in person at

Arrowhead Stadium, the fans are called the "Sea of Red" because of the noise they make, their tendency to wear red Chiefs merchandise to support the team, and their sheer numbers.

6. Kansas City cornerback Mark McMillian received the nickname "Mighty Mouse" from teammates Andre Rison and Derrick Thomas because McMillian tended to make big plays during key moments. This was based on a well-known line in the Mighty Mouse cartoon theme song: "Here I come to save the day!"

7. The size and strength of the Chiefs' 1960s and 1970s defense were notable. This, combined with the bright red of Kansas City's jerseys, led the unit to be nicknamed the "Redwood Forest."

8. Knile Davis ran hard as a Chief running back and his powerful style combined with the fact that a popular Kansas City amusement park, called Worlds of Fun, had a water rafting ride named "Fury of the Nile", as in the Egyptian river, led to the easy play on words of calling Davis "Fury of the Knile."

9. During his time in Kansas City, wide receiver Andre Rison celebrated his scoring plays by miming the shooting of webs out of his wrists, like a popular superhero. For this reason, he quickly became known as "Spiderman."

10. Chiefs' center Barry Richardson was not well thought of for his blocking ability. Richardson was given the nickname "Ole'," a reference to the bullfighting move

where a matador whisks himself and his cape out of the way to allow the bull to charge past.

CHAPTER 4:

THE QUARTERBACKS

QUIZ TIME!

1. Which of these Chiefs quarterbacks was sacked by opponents 195 times, the most during his Kansas City career?

   a. Trent Green
   b. Len Dawson
   c. Alex Smith
   d. Bill Kenney

2. Patrick Mahomes holds the top four spots on the Chiefs' all-time list of most passing touchdowns thrown in a season.

   a. True
   b. False

3. Which quarterback has thrown the most interceptions in Chiefs' franchise history?

   a. Steve DeBerg
   b. Mike Livingston

c. Len Dawson

d. Steve Bono

4. Who is the Chiefs' all-time career leader in passing yards?

    a. Len Dawson

    b. Patrick Mahomes

    c. Alex Smith

    d. Trent Green

5. Which Chiefs player set the franchise record for most passing yards in a season by a Kansas City quarterback with 5097 yards and is the only one ever to crack 5000?

    a. Bill Kenney

    b. Joe Montana

    c. Steve DeBerg

    d. Patrick Mahomes

6. How many former Chiefs quarterbacks have been elected to the Pro Football Hall of Fame?

    a. One – Len Dawson

    b. Two – Len Dawson and Joe Montana

    c. Three – Len Dawson, Joe Montana, and Warren Moon

    d. Four – Len Dawson, Joe Montana, Warren Moon, and Patrick Mahomes

7. Trent Green played more games at QB for the Chiefs than any other player.

    a. True

    b. False

8. Two journeyman Chiefs quarterbacks have played for seven NFL teams, more than any other franchise leaders. Who were these well-traveled players?

   a. Matt Cassel and Steve DeBerg
   b. Bill Kenney and Trent Green
   c. Mike Livingston and Alex Smith
   d. Elvis Grbac and Rich Gannon

9. Which of the following Chiefs is NOT tied for the franchise record as the youngest player in the team's history to start at quarterback, at just 22 years old?

   a. Patrick Mahomes
   b. Todd Blackledge
   c. Steve Fuller
   d. Tyler Thigpen

10. Which Kansas City quarterback was sent to the Washington Redskins to make way for new QB Patrick Mahomes after leading the Chiefs to the playoffs three years in a row?

   a. Nick Foles
   b. Matt Cassel
   c. Alex Smith
   d. Tyler Thigpen

11. How old was Chiefs' legend Len Dawson when he retired from playing in the NFL?

   a. 28 years old
   b. 33 years old

c. 37 years old

d. 40 years old

12. Chiefs QB Patrick Mahomes named previous QB Alex Smith as the godfather when his daughter Cynthia Mahomes was born in 2018.

a. True

b. False

13. Which Chiefs quarterback once broke his finger toward the end of the regular season and had to play a playoff game with a rod inserted into that finger to keep it from bending?

a. Steve DeBerg

b. Joe Montana

c. Matt Cassel

d. Trent Green

14. Which of the following is NOT a baseball fact about Chiefs superstar quarterback Patrick Mahomes?

a. His father played Major League baseball with several different clubs in the 1990s and 2000s.

b. He is a part-owner of Major League Baseball's Kansas City Royals.

c. He once hit a home run off of future Cy Young Award winner Shane Bieber.

d. He was drafted by Major League Baseball's Detroit Tigers in a late round in 2014.

15. Alex Smith holds the franchise record for most rushing yards in a season by a quarterback, which he set in 2015. How many yards did he rack up?

    a. 386
    b. 498
    c. 612
    d. 844

16. Kansas City star Joe Montana has won both a College Football National Championship and an NFL Super Bowl Championship.

    a. True
    b. False

17. For which two NFL teams did Chiefs icon Len Dawson play before ending up with the Kansas City franchise for over a decade?

    a. Detroit Lions and New York Giants
    b. Washington Redskins and San Francisco 49ers
    c. Pittsburgh Steelers and Cleveland Browns
    d. Green Bay Packers and Chicago Bears

18. Only one athlete in the history of sports signed a playing contract larger than the 12-year, $503 million contract inked by Kansas City's Patrick Mahomes. Which athlete exceeded this blockbuster deal with a $673 million deal?

    a. Outfielder Mike Trout with the Los Angeles Angels in Major League Baseball
    b. Forward Giannis Antetokounmpo with the Milwaukee Bucks in the National Basketball Association

c. Driver Kimi Raikkonen with Ferrari in Formula One Racing

d. Forward Lionel Messi with FC Barcelona in Spain's La Liga

19. How many times did prolific Chiefs' quarterback Len Dawson throw for 30 or more touchdowns in a single season?

a. One time
b. Two times
c. Four times
d. Seven times

20. Among quarterbacks who have started at least five games with Kansas City, quarterback Ron Jaworski has the highest interception percentage, with 8.2% of his passes thrown being picked off.

a. True
b. False

QUIZ ANSWERS

1. D – Bill Kenney

2. B – False

3. C – Len Dawson

4. A – Len Dawson

5. D – Patrick Mahomes

6. C – Three – Len Dawson, Joe Montana, and Warren Moon

7. B – False

8. A – Matt Cassel and Steve DeBerg

9. D – Tyler Thigpen

10. C – Alex Smith

11. D – 40 years old

12. B – False

13. A – Steve DeBerg

14. C – He once hit a home run off of future Cy Young Award winner Shane Bieber.

15. B – 498

16. A – True

17. C – Pittsburgh Steelers and Cleveland Browns

18. D – Forward Lionel Messi with FC Barcelona in Spain's La Liga

19. A – One time

20. A – True

DID YOU KNOW?

1. Trent Green owns the longest passing play in Chiefs' history. He dropped back and found receiver Marc Boerigter for a 99-yard touchdown toss in 2002 that helped Kansas City beat the San Diego Chargers 24-22.

2. No Chiefs quarterback who started for the entire season has ever been able to complete 70% of his passes in a season. The most accurate field general was Alex Smith, who came the closest in 2016 and 2017, when he hit 67%.

3. Steve Fuller could have used some better blocking when he became the Chiefs QB in 1980. He was sacked a whopping 49 times when he dropped back to pass, the highest total in Kansas City history.

4. Outside of the 1987 strike season, no quarterbacks have played their entire NFL careers with Kansas City. Current quarterback Patrick Mahomes has not played anywhere else in his NFL career and is under contract with the team until 2032, but it remains to be seen if he will retire as a Chief.

5. Quarterback Len Dawson has the longest tenure as Chiefs QB. He started playing for the team in 1962 and did not give up the position until 1975, after 183 games played with Kansas City.

6. Doug Hudson played just five minutes in one game at quarterback for the Kansas City Chiefs, and it was

memorable for the wrong reasons. He did not complete any passes, and his only NFL statistic is a safety, after Hudson struggled with a handoff and recovered the dropped ball in his own end zone.

7. Kansas City's Patrick Mahomes is the only player ever to pass for over 5000 yards in a season in both the NCAA and NFL. Mahomes hit 5052 yards for Texas Tech in 2016 and topped that against a higher level of competition with 5097 yards for the Chiefs in 2018.

8. Quarterback Trent Green had an explosive year in 2003, including a notable achievement while on the losing end of a playoff game against the Indianapolis Colts. For the first time in an NFL playoff game, Green and Colts QB Peyton Manning both led their offenses through a full four quarters without a single punt.

9. In 1989, Kansas City put two players on the field who very nearly set a record. Quarterback Ron Jaworski, who was 38, took snaps from center Mike Webster, who was 37. Their combined age made them the second oldest duo in these positions in NFL history, trailing only the Raiders' battery of George Blanda, who was 46, and Jim Otto, who was 36.

10. Chiefs' quarterback Todd Blackledge had an outstanding career in college. As a student, Blackledge made first-team Academic All-American, finished his degree with a 3.8 grade point average, and was later inducted into the Academic All-America Hall of Fame.

CHAPTER 5:

THE PASS CATCHERS

QUIZ TIME!

1. Three pass catchers have recorded over 50 career touchdown catches for the Chiefs. Which one of the following got stuck at 49 and didn't make the cut?

   a. Wide receiver Otis Taylor

   b. Tight end Tony Gonzalez

   c. Split end Chris Burford

   d. Wide receiver Stephone Paige

2. No one in Chiefs history is within 300 receptions of Tony Gonzalez at the top of Kansas City's record book.

   a. True

   b. False

3. Two players are tied as the Chiefs single season leader in receiving touchdowns scored, with 15. Who are they?

   a. Split end Chris Burford and tight end Travis Kelce

   b. Wide receiver Otis Taylor and tight end Tony Gonzalez

   c. Wide receivers Tyreek Hill and Dwayne Bowe

d. Wide receivers Stephone Paige and Derrick Alexander

4. Who holds the all-time career franchise record for receiving yardage with 10,940 yards?

   a. Wide receiver Henry Marshall
   b. Tight end Tony Gonzalez
   c. Wide receiver Dwayne Bowe
   d. Tight end Travis Kelce

5. In 2016 against the Denver Broncos, Chiefs wide receiver Tyreek Hill became the first player in many years to score a rushing touchdown, receiving touchdown, and kickoff return touchdown in the same game. Who was the last player before Hill to accomplish this feat?

   a. Running back Jim Brown of the Cleveland Browns in 1961
   b. Wide receiver Lance Alworth of the San Diego Chargers in 1963
   c. Running back Gale Sayers of the Chicago Bears in 1965
   d. Wide receiver Billy Johnson of the Houston Oilers in 1974

6. Only one Chief with at least 100 receptions has averaged 18 yards per catch over his career. Which player has shown this amazing big play ability?

   a. Wide receiver Chris Carson
   b. Wide receiver Otis Taylor
   c. Tight end Travis Kelce
   d. Wide receiver Derrick Alexander

7. Kansas City legend Tony Gonzalez, who grew up in California, once shared an Orange County High School Athlete of the Year Award with superstar golfer Tiger Woods.

   a. True
   b. False

8. Which Chiefs pass-catcher has played more NFL games with the franchise than any other player in the position group?

   a. Tight end Jonathan Hayes
   b. Wide receiver Henry Marshall
   c. Wide receiver Stephone Paige
   d. Tight end Tony Gonzalez

9. Three pass catchers have over 500 career receptions for the Kansas City Chiefs. Which of the following players is NOT among that club?

   a. Split end Chris Burford
   b. Tight end Tony Gonzalez
   c. Wide receiver Dwayne Bowe
   d. Tight end Travis Kelce

10. Despite all his accomplishments, Dante Hall has more career fumbles than any other Chiefs wide receiver. How many times did he cough up the ball?

    a. 11 times
    b. 14 times
    c. 17 times
    d. 21 times

11. At the end of the 2020 NFL season, the Chiefs had 11 wide receivers under contract for 2021. Which one of those wide receivers was the only one with a base salary over $1 million?

   a. Byron Pringle
   b. Tyreek Hill
   c. Demarcus Robinson
   d. Mecole Hardman

12. Chiefs pass-catcher Carlos Carson was the first non-kicking player born in Mexico to suit up for an NFL team.

   a. True
   b. False

13. How many Chiefs tight ends have caught over 200 passes for the club during their careers?

   a. One – Tony Gonzalez
   b. Two – Tony Gonzalez and Travis Kelce
   c. Three – Tony Gonzalez, Travis Kelce, and Fred Arbanas
   d. Four – Tony Gonzalez, Travis Kelce, Fred Arbanas, and Walter White

14. Which two teammates posted the highest combined receiving yardage total in a season for the Chiefs, with 2815 altogether?

   a. Tight end Travis Kelce and wide receiver Tyreek Hill in 2018
   b. Tight end Tony Gonzalez and wide receiver Derrick Alexander in 2004

c. Wide receivers Carlos Carson and Stephone Paige in 1987

d. Wide receivers Eddie Kennison and Derrick Alexander in 2004

15. Which of the following is NOT a fact about Chiefs wide receiver Stephone Paige's amazing 309-yard receiving game against the San Diego Chargers in 1985?

a. Paige had never recorded even 100 receiving yards in a game before it happened,

b. Paige set an NFL record in this game, and it remains one of only five 300-yard games in NFL history,

c. Paige racked up all of his yardage on only 8 total receptions during the game,

d. Paige failed to record a touchdown, twice getting tackled inside the 5-yard line after long runs,

16. In a very fast start against the New York Jets in a 2017 game, Kansas City tight end Travis Kelce had two touchdowns and 90 yards receiving…after just two minutes and 46 seconds had run off the clock in the first quarter.

a. True

b. False

17. Hall-of-Fame Chiefs tight end Tony Gonzalez squared off against which Hall-of-Fame linebacker on the television show *Lip Sync Battle*, where Gonzalez performed iconic songs "Whip It" and the "Humpty Dance," but lost the battle?

a. Brian Urlacher of the Chicago Bears

b. Kevin Greene of the Pittsburgh Steelers

c. Ray Lewis of the Baltimore Ravens

d. Junior Seau of the San Diego Chargers

18. Which Chief recorded the most catches in one season for the team, with 105?

a. Tight end Tony Gonzalez

b. Wide receiver Jeremy Maclin

c. Running back Priest Holmes

d. Tight end Travis Kelce

19. Which two teammates posted the highest touchdown reception total in a season for the Chiefs, converting 26 passes into scores?

a. Split end Chris Burford and wide receiver Frank Jackson in 1964

b. Wide receivers Derrick Alexander and Marc Boerigter in 2003

c. Tight end Travis Kelce and wide receiver Tyreek Hill in 2020

d. Tight end Travis Kelce and wide receiver Tyreek Hill in 2018

20. Kansas City's Travis Kelce holds the NFL record for most receiving yards in a single season by a tight end, with 1416 yards in 2020.

a. True

b. False

QUIZ ANSWERS

1. D – Wide receiver Stephone Paige

2. A – True

3. C – Wide receivers Tyreek Hill and Dwayne Bowe

4. B – Tight end Tony Gonzalez

5. C – Running back Gale Sayers of the Chicago Bears in 1965

6. A – Wide receiver Chris Carson

7. A – True

8. D – Tight end Tony Gonzalez

9. A – Split end Chris Burford

10. C – 17 times

11. A – Byron Pringle

12. B – False

13. B – Two – Tony Gonzalez and Travis Kelce

14. A – Tight end Travis Kelce and wide receiver Tyreek Hill in 2018

15. D – Paige failed to record a touchdown, twice getting tackled inside the 5-yard line after long runs.

16. A – True

17. C – Ray Lewis of the Baltimore Ravens

18. D – Tight end Travis Kelce

19. C – Tight end Travis Kelce and wide receiver Tyreek Hill in 2020

20. A – True

DID YOU KNOW?

1. Chiefs' icon Tony Gonzalez ranks third on the all-time list for career receptions in the NFL. Gonzalez racked up 1325 catches, behind only wide receivers Jerry Rice and Larry Fitzgerald. Gonzalez is almost 100 catches beyond the closest tight end, Jason Witten, who ranks fourth.

2. The single-game record for most receptions in Kansas City Chiefs history was set by a tight end, Tony Gonzalez, who reeled in 14 passes against the San Diego Chargers in 2005 to set the mark.

3. Star Chiefs' tight end Travis Kelce is the brother of Philadelphia Eagles center Jason Kelce. Both brothers have excelled in the NFL, making first-team All-Pro three times apiece. In 2018, both brothers made the squad in the same year.

4. During the 2010 NFL season, Chiefs wide receiver Dwayne Bowe set a franchise record for most consecutive games with a touchdown catch, as he scored in seven straight games before being voted to the Pro Bowl and being selected to the All-Pro second team.

5. Chiefs wide receiver Otis Taylor was a star for the team and later went on to become a scout for the franchise. During the NFL strike in 1987, when Taylor showed up to work, Chiefs' linebacker Jack Del Rio did not recognize him and thought Taylor was crossing the picket line,

which led to Del Rio assaulting Taylor and eventually led to an out-of-court settlement.

6. Two players have recorded 4 receiving touchdowns in a single game for the Chiefs. Frank Jackson accomplished this feat in 1964, and more recently, Jamaal Charles matched the mark, as a running back, no less, in 2013.

7. While dining at a restaurant, legendary Chiefs tight end Tony Gonzalez saved the life of a fellow patron who was choking on his food. Gonzalez performed the Heimlich maneuver to dislodge the obstruction and later learned that the diner was a fan of the rival San Diego Chargers.

8. Tight end Fred Arbanas was one tough player for the Kansas City Chiefs. After being attacked by two assailants in 1965, Arbanas lost vision in one of his eyes but continued to play for the Chiefs for five more years, even making an All-Star team in one of them.

9. The Chiefs' second leading receiver of all time, Henry Marshall, played every game of his NFL career for Kansas City. Marshall suited up for the squad for 165 games over more than a decade, from 1976 through 1987, and tallied all of his yards without ever notching a 1000-yard season.

10. It is always a challenge to compare players from different eras with each other, but most experts agree that Chiefs WR Tyreek Hill is at least in the top 10 fastest players in NFL history. Technology was not always available to measure this accurately in earlier seasons, but Hill was definitely the fastest NFL player in 2016, recording a game speed of 22.77 miles per hour.

CHAPTER 6:

RUNNING WILD

QUIZ TIME!

1. Who holds the Chiefs single season rushing yardage record with 1789 yards?

   a. Priest Holmes
   b. Christian Okoye
   c. Larry Johnson
   d. Jamaal Charles

2. It is a Chiefs tradition for every running back to tap his helmet against the helmets of the starting offensive linemen following the warmup before a game.

   a. True
   b. False

3. Which running back accumulated the most carries for Kansas City without scoring a rushing TD?

   a. Dexter McCluster
   b. Joe Delaney
   c. Harvey Williams
   d. Larry Moriarty

4. Which of the following is NOT a fact about quirky Chiefs running back Christian Okoye?

   a. He starred in a Nintendo video game called Super Tecmo Bowl in which he was able to break 86 tackles in a single play.
   b. He married three different women at the same time in his home country, Nigeria.
   c. He had never played a game of football until age 23.
   d. He is the president of the California Sports Hall of Fame, which he also founded.

5. How many running backs have carried the ball over 1000 times for the Chiefs?

   a. 1
   b. 2
   c. 5
   d. 8

6. No Chiefs running back with at least 16 games played has averaged over 100 yards per game during his career. Priest Holmes is the closest; what is his average?

   a. 93.4 yards
   b. 95.1 yards
   c. 96.8 yards
   d. 99.4 yards

7. Priest Holmes has 76 career rushing touchdowns with the Chiefs. which is more than the next two highest Kansas City running backs combined.

a. True

b. False

8. In which season did Jamaal Charles record an astonishing 6.4 yards per carry for Kansas City?

a. 2008

b. 2010

c. 2012

d. 2014

9. Which Kansas City running back with at least 300 carries has the highest career yards gained per attempt, with 5.5?

a. Priest Holmes

b. Larry Johnson

c. Kareem Hunt

d. Jamaal Charles

10. Kareem Hunt recorded his first NFL touchdown against which team?

a. Cleveland Browns

b. Kansas City Chiefs

c. San Francisco 49ers

d. New England Patriots

11. How many of the Chiefs' top 10 seasons for rushing touchdowns were recorded by the great Priest Holmes?

a. 0

b. 1

c. 3

d. 6

12. When he was 10 years old, future Chiefs running back Jamaal Charles competed in track and field in the Special Olympics.

   a. True
   b. False

13. Which Kansas City running back has the most career fumbles, with 42?

   a. Ed Podolak
   b. Larry Johnson
   c. Mike Garrett
   d. Herman Heard

14. Which Chief had the highest single season rushing yards per game, with 115.4?

   a. Larry Johnson
   b. Priest Holmes
   c. Christian Okoye
   d. Marcus Allen

15. Which Chiefs rusher had an incredible year with the club at age 37, setting the NFL record as the oldest player to score over 10 touchdowns in a season?

   a. Priest Holmes
   b. Tony Reed
   c. Marcus Allen
   d. Ed Podolak

16. Legendary Chiefs running back Marcus Allen married his wife Kathryn at the home of infamous Buffalo Bills running back O.J. Simpson.

    a. True
    b. False

17. Which of the following is NOT a fact about enigmatic Chiefs running back Larry Johnson?

    a. He has tweeted that Los Angeles Lakers star LeBron James was complicit in the death of fellow Laker Kobe Bryant.
    b. He has been suspended by the NFL for berating the calls of referees during games.
    c. He has posted social media material supporting Adolph Hitler and denying the Holocaust.
    d. He has been arrested five times on assault charges, and once for disturbing the peace.

18. Original Dallas Texans running back Abner Haynes still owns all of the following Chiefs franchise records, except for which one?

    a. Most total points scored in a single game, with 30
    b. Most total yards gained in a career, with 8442
    c. Most touchdowns scored in a single game, with 5
    d. Longest rush on a single play, with a 98-yard gain

19. Only five NFL running backs have ever carried the ball more than 400 times in a single season. Which Chiefs

rusher had the heaviest workload of all, logging 416 rushing attempts, the league record?

    a. Christian Okoye in 1989

    b. Larry Johnson in 2006

    c. Priest Holmes in 2001

    d. Jamaal Charles in 2012

20. As a rookie in 2017, Kareem Hunt led the NFL in rushing yards with 1327.

    a. True

    b. False

QUIZ ANSWERS

1. C – Larry Johnson

2. B – False

3. D – Larry Moriarty

4. B – He married three different women at the same time in his home country, Nigeria.

5. C – 5

6. A – 93.4 yards

7. B – False

8. B –2010

9. D – Jamaal Charles

10. D – New England Patriots

11. C – 3

12. A – True

13. A – Ed Podolak

14. B – Priest Holmes

15. C – Marcus Allen

16. A – True

17. B – He has been suspended by the NFL for berating the calls of referees during games.

18. D – Longest rush on a single play, with a 98-yard gain

19. B – Larry Johnson in 2006

20. A – True

DID YOU KNOW?

1. After 50 years, Kansas City running back Ed Podolak still stands atop the NFL record books for most total yards gained in a playoff game. Facing the Miami Dolphins, Podolak rushed for 85 yards, reeled in 110 receiving yards, and added 155 yards on kick returns. His 350 total yards easily bests every playoff game performance before and since.

2. Ten times in NFL history, a running back has scored 20 or more rushing touchdowns in a single season. Three of those ten times, the rusher has been a Chief. Kansas City's Priest Holmes accomplished the feat in back-to-back seasons in 2002 and 2003 (21 and 27 touchdowns), and Larry Johnson also reached that threshold with an even 20 touchdowns in 2005.

3. Despite a rich history of rushing leaders, only one running back who has played for the Chiefs has been enshrined in the Pro Football Hall of Fame. That is the great Marcus Allen, who was elected in 2003.

4. Not only is Marcus Allen in the Pro Football and College Football Halls of Fame, but he is also the only player ever to win the NCAA Championship, the Heisman Trophy, the NFL MVP Award, the Super Bowl, and the Super Bowl MVP Award.

5. The very talented Jamaal Charles was unfortunate with his history of injuries, tearing his ACL twice while playing with the Chiefs. The first time, he missed a year but came back to make second-team All-Pro the following season. The second time, he was released by the club.

6. Although he had a stellar start to his NFL career with Kansas City, running back Kareem Hunt was cut by the team after less than two full seasons, because of a video that surfaced showing Hunt kicking a woman. Chiefs' owner Clark Hunt released the talented but troubled running back and Hunt eventually signed with the Cleveland Browns.

7. After he retired from the NFL, former Chiefs' rusher Thomas Jones began an acting career under the name Thomas Q. Jones, and appeared in such popular productions as the movie *Straight Outta Compton* and the television shows *Shameless*, *Luke Cage*, and *Hawaii Five-O*.

8. In 2005, running back Larry Johnson set the Kansas City franchise record for most rushing yards in a season with 1750 and was named team MVP. Even more impressive? Johnson did this while starting only 9 of the Chiefs' 16 regular-season games.

9. Star Chiefs running back Kareem Hunt had quite the introduction to the NFL. In his first game, against the New England Patriots, Hunt fumbled on his very first carry. Luckily, he did not let the bad start to his career get him down and he finished the game with 3 TDs.

10. Running back Stone Johnson once held the world record in the 200-meter sprint and Kansas City was excited to sign him in 1963. Tragically, the speedster fractured a vertebra while returning a Houston Oilers kick in a preseason game. Johnson died from the injury less than two weeks later.

CHAPTER 7:

IN THE TRENCHES

QUIZ TIME!

1. Which of the following is NOT a fact about Kansas City defensive end Neil Smith?

    a. Smith modeled his celebration for sacking an opposing quarterback on the baseball swing of Kansas City Royals legend George Brett.
    b. Smith played for three teams in his NFL career, all of which were in the AFC West Division.
    c. Smith enjoyed the game of basketball and frequently scrimmaged with the University of Kansas Jayhawks team during the NFL offseason.
    d. Smith was part owner of an Arena Football League team called the Kansas City Brigade.

2. The 2016 Kansas City Chiefs hold the NFL record for the heaviest combined weight of all starting offensive and defensive linemen.

    a. True
    b. False

3. Who is the Chiefs' all-time franchise leader in sacks, with 126.5?

    a. Defensive end Neil Smith
    b. Linebacker Justin Houston
    c. Defensive end Jared Allen
    d. Linebacker Derrick Thomas

4. Which offensive lineman did the Chiefs select highest in the NFL entry draft, using a first overall pick to add the stout blocker to their team?

    a. Tackle Eric Fisher
    b. Guard Brian Jozwiak
    c. Tackle Francis Peay
    d. Guard Rod Walters

5. Which offensive lineman played more games on the offensive side of the Chiefs line of scrimmage than anyone else?

    a. Tackle Jim Tyrer
    b. Guard Will Shields
    c. Center Tim Grunhard
    d. Guard Ed Budde

6. Which defensive lineman played more games on the defensive side of the Chiefs line of scrimmage than anyone else?

    a. End Jerry Mays
    b. End Neil Smith
    c. End Tamba Hali
    d. Tackle Buck Buchanan

7. While playing in college at Idaho State University, future Chiefs defensive end Jared Allen won an award named after former Kansas City legend Buck Buchanan, given to the best defensive player in Division I-AA each year.

   a. True
   b. False

8. Which Chiefs defender leads the team in most career forced fumbles, with 41?

   a. Tamba Hali
   b. Neil Smith
   c. Derrick Thomas
   d. Jared Allen

9. Which defender created the most turnovers for Kansas City by scooping up an opponent's fumble 19 times?

   a. Dan Saleaumua
   b. Neil Smith
   c. Mike Bell
   d. Derrick Thomas

10. Defensive end Dave Lindstrom bought into the restaurant business after his career with the Chiefs, owning four Kansas City locations for which popular fast-food franchise?

   a. Burger King
   b. Taco Bell
   c. Jack in the Box
   d. Panera Bread

11. Chiefs' mainstay Will Shields played over 200 NFL games as a right guard with the club. Where does he rank in games played all-time for Kansas City?

    a. First
    b. Second
    c. Tied for fifth
    d. Tied for eighth

12. Chiefs' center Casey Wiegmann married another Kansas native, Danni Boatwright, who was known for wearing Chiefs' gear and flaunting her fandom during her time on the reality television show *Survivor: Guatemala*, on which Boatwright won $1 million.

    a. True
    b. False

13. Which current Chiefs defensive lineman has the longest tenure in Kansas City?

    a. Defensive end Frank Clark
    b. Defensive tackle Jarran Reed
    c. Defensive end Taco Charlton
    d. Defensive tackle Chris Jones

14. Which of these institutions does Chiefs offensive lineman Will Shields NOT belong to:

    a. The College Football Hall of Fame
    b. The State of Kansas Hall of Fame
    c. The Kansas City Chiefs Hall of Fame
    d. The Pro Football Hall of Fame

15. Chiefs offensive tackle Mitchell Schwartz had the longest active playing streak among NFL players until 2019 when he injured his knee against the Tennessee Titans. How many consecutive snaps did his streak encompass before it ended?

    a. 3, 105 snaps
    b. 4, 933 snaps
    c. 6, 207 snaps
    d. 7, 894 snaps

16. In 2020, Kansas City offensive tackle Eric Fisher caught the first touchdown pass thrown to a first overall draft pick since Keyshawn Johnson caught one in 2006.

    a. True
    b. False

17. Which of the following is NOT a fact about unique Chiefs guard Laurent Duvernay-Tardif?

    a. He was so talented that head coach Andy Reid allowed him to practice just once a week, providing time to pursue his other interests rather than give up football altogether.
    b. He was the 10th player in NFL history to be drafted from a Canadian University.
    c. He petitioned the NFL to include "M.D." on his jersey name, because of his medical degree.
    d. He was a reporter for a major national network who covered the 2018 Winter Olympics during the NFL off-season.

18. What was the real first name of Chiefs Hall-of-Fame defensive tackle Buck Buchanan?

    a. Buck
    b. LaBradford
    c. Roscoe-Benjamin
    d. Junious

19. Chiefs defensive end Art Still went to three straight Pro Bowls from 1980 through 1982 before becoming a vegetarian, losing 30 pounds, and missing the Pro Bowl in 1983. What happened to Still the following year, in 1984?

    a. He was cut by the Chiefs in training camp and saw his NFL career come to an end.
    b. He maintained the vegetarian diet, lost 20 more pounds, and returned to the Pro Bowl.
    c. He switched back to eating meat, regained the weight, and was back in the Pro Bowl again.
    d. He was replaced as a starter by star Derrick Thomas and relegated to a backup role.

20. In retirement, Chiefs defensive end Jared Allen formed his own team in the sport of competitive curling, which consisted of himself and three other former NFL players.

    a. True
    b. False

QUIZ ANSWERS

1. C – Smith enjoyed the game of basketball and frequently scrimmaged with the University of Kansas Jayhawks team during the NFL offseason.

2. B – False

3. D – Linebacker Derrick Thomas

4. A – Tackle Eric Fisher

5. B – Guard Will Shields

6. D – Tackle Buck Buchanan

7. A – True

8. C – Derrick Thomas

9. D – Derrick Thomas

10. A – Burger King

11. B – Second

12. A – True

13. D – Defensive tackle Chris Jones

14. B – The State of Kansas Hall of Fame

15. D – 7, 894 snaps

16. A – True

17. A – He was so talented that head coach Andy Reid allowed him to practice just once a week, providing time

to pursue his other interests rather than give up football altogether.

18. D – Junious

19. C – He switched back to eating meat, regained the weight, and was back in the Pro Bowl again.

20. A – True

DID YOU KNOW?

1. Guard Will Shields played for the Chiefs, only and always. Shields never suited up for another NFL franchise and never missed a game during his 14-season career. His 231 straight starts are a record for an NFL guard.

2. Center E.J. Holub was not just a stud on the Chiefs' offensive line. Holub also played linebacker, once staying on the field for 58 minutes, out of a possible 60, and becoming the only two-way player to be a starter on both sides of the ball in multiple Super Bowls.

3. Kansas City offensive tackle Jim Tyrer was selected as an All-Pro six times during his career, which is the most for any NFL player who is NOT enshrined in the Pro Football Hall of Fame.

4. Brian Waters notched a rare achievement in 2004 when he was chosen as the AFC Offensive Player of the Week after a game against the Atlanta Falcons in which Kansas City rushed for an NFL record 8 touchdowns. Waters is the only offensive lineman ever to win this particular award.

5. Former Chiefs guard Tom Condon not only spent a decade with the team but also served two years as the president of the NFL Players Association. In retirement, Condon became one of the biggest agents in professional sports, representing stars like Peyton Manning, Drew Brees, and even Chiefs' quarterback Alex Smith.

6. Brothers Rich and Gary Baldinger not only both made it to the NFL, but both made it to the same team as well. From 1986 through 1988, offensive lineman Rich would line up across from defensive lineman Gary in practice and the two would battle along the line of scrimmage.

7. Nose tackle Bill Maas was a pioneer for the Kansas City Chiefs. Not only was he the first Chiefs player to win Rookie of the Year, but Maas was also the first Kansas City nose tackle ever elected to the Pro Bowl.

8. Guards Ed and Brad Budde have an interesting distinction, as they are the only father and son duo to be drafted in the first round by the same NFL team. Kansas City took Ed with the 8th overall pick in 1963 and chose his son Brad with the 11th pick in 1980.

9. Chiefs offensive tackle Mitchell Schwartz and his brother Geoff, a Chiefs guard, did not play in Kansas City at the same time but were the first Jewish brothers to play in the NFL since 1923, and they once played against each other when Geoff was a Chief and Mitchell was a Cleveland Brown.

10. Kansas City guard Laurent Duvernay-Tardif graduated from medical school at McGill University. He was only the fourth NFL player with a degree in that field. In 2020, Duvernay-Tardif gave up his lucrative Chiefs contract to opt-out of the NFL season and work as a medical orderly, fighting COVID-19 during the global pandemic caused by the virus.

CHAPTER 8:

THE BACK SEVEN

QUIZ TIME!

1. Which Chiefs cornerback is the franchise's all-time leader in interceptions with 58?

    a. Brandon Carr
    b. Albert Lewis
    c. Emmitt Thomas
    d. Kevin Ross

2. During the 2010s poker craze, members of Kansas City's secondary and linebacking corps held a weekly game where, rather than playing for money, the losers had to tweet embarrassing things about themselves or flattering things about the winners.

    a. True
    b. False

3. One Kansas City Chief player holds the team's lead for most interceptions returned for a touchdown, with 6. Who is he?

a. Cornerback Emmitt Thomas

b. Linebacker Derrick Johnson

c. Safety Jim Kearney

d. Linebacker Bobby Bell

4. Sacks are usually not a high priority for defensive backs in Kansas City coaching systems, which means that defensive back Ron Parker is the Chiefs career leader in sacks by a DB with which small number?

a. 3

b. 5

c. 8

d. 12

5. The initials in popular Chiefs defensive back J.C. Pearson's name stand for what?

a. Jayice

b. Jonathan Charles

c. Jason Christopher

d. Jamaal Chadwick

6. The most tackles ever made by a Chiefs player in a single season is 162. Which player accomplished this feat?

a. Linebacker Gary Spani

b. Linebacker Jim Lynch

c. Linebacker Mike Maslowski

d. Safety Eric Berry

7. Hall-of-Fame linebacker Willie Lanier's tackles were so violent that Kansas City's equipment manager occasionally

added extra padding to the *outside* of Lanier's helmet, to protect opposing players from injury.

a. True

b. False

8. Which of the following is NOT a fact about quirky linebacker Sherrill Headrick, who was a star on the original Dallas Texans team and played with the Chiefs franchise for seven years?

a. He remained on the field to play despite injuries as severe as a broken vertebra in his neck and a broken bone sticking out of his finger.

b. He owned a fried chicken restaurant franchise with locations throughout the state of Texas.

c. He refused to travel by plane and would leave Kansas City early for long road trips so that he would have time to make it to other cities by car or train.

d. He was a great card player and ranked as a Diamond Life Master in the American Contract Bridge League.

9. How did linebacker Derrick Thomas suffer the injury that put an end to his NFL career?

a. He suffered a concussion while making a tackle on Denver Broncos running back Terrell Davis in a playoff game.

b. He was paralyzed from the waist down after crashing his vehicle on an icy road while not wearing his seatbelt.

c. He was shot in the leg during an armed robbery at the team's hotel in San Francisco.

d. He broke a vertebra while diving into shallow water on a Caribbean vacation.

10. What was the name of the restaurant that Chiefs' linebacker Bobby Bell opened in Kansas City after his playing days were over?

    a. "Burnt Ends"
    b. "The Chiefs Chophouse"
    c. "The Linebacker Lounge"
    d. "Bobby Bell's Bar-B-Que"

11. Chiefs' mainstay Derrick Thomas played 169 NFL games with the club. Where does he rank in games played all-time for Kansas City?

    a. Tied for 4th
    b. 9th
    c. Tied for 15th
    d. 22nd

12. Kansas City great Emmitt Thomas played cornerback only for the Chiefs during his 13-year NFL career. However, in retirement, Thomas coached for six other NFL franchises for almost 30 years before landing a job as Kansas City's defensive backs coach.

    a. True
    b. False

13. Which of the following is NOT a fact about Kansas City Hall-of-Fame safety Johnny Robinson?

    a. He played in both the longest game and longest championship game in NFL history.

b. Robinson is one of just 20 athletes who played in the AFL for its entire decade-long existence.

c. Robinson was the only member of the Chiefs ever to be paid as both a player and an assistant coach during the same season.

d. Robinson became a scout for the Chiefs after his retirement as a player.

14. Which of these current Chiefs defensive backs has been with the team for seven seasons, the longest current tenure in Kansas City's back seven?

a. Safety Tyrann Mathieu

b. Safety Daniel Sorenson

c. Cornerback Charvarius Ward

d. Cornerback DeAndre Baker

15. Which of the following statements about Chiefs' safety Eric Berry is NOT true:

a. He won the NFL's Comeback Player of the Year Award in 2015 after missing a season due to Hodgkin's lymphoma.

b. He was named to all-decade teams in both high school and the NFL.

c. As a rookie, he became the highest-paid safety in the history of the NFL.

d. He was a basketball star at the University of Tennessee and was drafted by the NBA's Atlanta Hawks.

16. Longtime Chiefs linebacker Tamba Hali learned Brazilian jiu-jitsu through the teaching of the legendary Gracie family and worked his way up to a purple belt.

    a. True
    b. False

17. Linebacker Mike Maslowski not only holds the Chiefs record for most tackles in a season but also holds the NFL Europe record for most tackles in a season, which he set with which club before joining Kansas City?

    a. Frankfurt Galaxy
    b. Scottish Claymores
    c. Amsterdam Admirals
    d. Barcelona Dragons

18. How old was Hall-of-Fame Chiefs linebacker Bobby Bell when he earned his degree in parks and recreation at the University of Minnesota?

    a. 16
    b. 34
    c. 58
    d. 74

19. One Chiefs defender set the NFL record with 7 sacks in a single game against the Seattle Seahawks. Which defender was this?

    a. Linebacker Derrick Thomas
    b. Safety Eric Berry
    c. Linebacker Justin Houston
    d. Linebacker Gary Spani

20. Hall-of-Fame Chiefs safety Johnny Robinson was also talented enough to win national high school and college SEC tennis titles at LSU. Robinson's brother Tommy was his doubles partner, and his father Dub was the school's tennis coach.

    a. True
    b. False

QUIZ ANSWERS

1. C – Emmitt Thomas

2. B – False

3. D – Linebacker Bobby Bell

4. C – 8

5. A – Jayice

6. C – Linebacker Mike Maslowski

7. A – True

8. C – He refused to travel by plane and would leave Kansas City early for long road trips so that he would have time to make it to other cities by car or train.

9. B – He was paralyzed from the waist down after crashing his vehicle on an icy road while not wearing his seatbelt.

10. D – "Bobby Bell's Bar-B-Que"

11. C – Tied for 15th

12. A – True

13. C – Robinson was the only member of the Chiefs ever to be paid as both a player and an assistant coach during the same season.

14. B – Safety Daniel Sorenson

15. D – He was a basketball star at the University of Tennessee and was drafted by the NBA's Atlanta Hawks.

16. A – True

17. D – Barcelona Dragons

18. D – 74

19. A – Linebacker Derrick Thomas

20. A – True

DID YOU KNOW?

1. Passes defended is a stat that the NFL began using at the turn of the 21st century. Cornerback Brandon Flowers has dominated the statistic for the Chiefs, having recorded a dozen more than his closest competition, defensive back Eric Warfield.

2. Hall-of-Fame linebacker Willie Lanier was revered in his time and far beyond. Lanier was named to the NFL's 75th Anniversary All-Time Team and 25 years later, with a host of new players to choose from, the Kansas City star was *still* included on the NFL's 100th Anniversary All-Time Team.

3. Linebacker Derrick Johnson is the all-time leading tackler for the Chiefs franchise. Johnson played in Kansas City for 13 seasons and racked up 1151 tackles during that time.

4. Longtime Chiefs defensive back Daniel Sorenson signed with the team as an undrafted free agent. His brother, quarterback Brad Sorenson, was taken in the 7th round of the 2013 NFL draft by the San Diego Chargers. Brad had bragging rights on draft position, but was out of the league in four years, whereas Daniel has been playing with Kansas City for seven years and counting.

5. Kansas City safety Eric Berry had equinophobia, which is the fear of horses. Berry would not go near the Chiefs'

mascot, a horse named Warpaint, because it triggered his anxiety.

6. Kansas City linebacker Derrick Thomas holds team records for most career safeties, with 3. Defensive tackles Dan Saleaumua and Bill Maas are tied behind him with 2 apiece.

7. Five defensive backs who have played for the Chiefs have been enshrined in the Pro Football Hall of Fame. The most recent were safety Johnny Robinson and cornerback Ty Law, who were elected in 2019.

8. Linebacker Justin Houston had a season for the ages in 2014. Houston finished the year with 22 sacks, the most ever for a Chief, and only half a sack behind NFL record-holder Michael Strahan of the New York Giants.

9. Chiefs' linebacker Tamba Hali had a noble goal that inspired him to greatness in his NFL career. At age 10, Hali had fled his home country of Liberia because of civil war, and he was determined to raise enough money to bring his mother safely to the United States of America as well.

10. The multi-talented Bobby Bell became a Hall-of-Fame linebacker for Kansas City. But Bell played halfback and quarterback in high school. In college, he played on the defensive line. In the NFL, he was regarded as perhaps the best long snapper of all time. Chiefs coach Hank Stram once remarked that Bell "could play all 22 positions on the field and play them well."

CHAPTER 9:

WHERE'D THEY COME FROM?

QUIZ TIME!

1. Where was legendary Chiefs tight end Tony Gonzalez born?

    a. Torrance, California

    b. Wichita, Kansas

    c. Honolulu, Hawaii

    d. Okeechobee, Florida

2. Quarterback Len Dawson, who played 14 years with the team, was born, and raised in Kansas City, Missouri.

    a. True

    b. False

3. In 1964, the Chiefs chose four players from one college. Which college was it?

    a. University of Michigan

    b. University of Texas

    c. University of Southern California

    d. University of Notre Dame

4. Which of the following superstars has NOT been involved in a trade between the Chiefs and San Francisco 49ers?

   a. Quarterback Joe Montana
   b. Defensive end Dee Ford
   c. Wide receiver Dwayne Bowe
   d. Quarterback Alex Smith

5. From which team did the Chiefs acquire useful linebacker Reggie Ragland in a 2017 swap?

   a. Buffalo Bills
   b. New Orleans Saints
   c. Cincinnati Bengals
   d. New York Jets

6. Which of the following is NOT an actual college program that Kansas City drafted a player from during the 1987 NFL draft?

   a. Azusa Pacific University Cougars
   b. Catawba College Indians
   c. Nicholls State University Colonels
   d. Crystal Lake University Sharks

7. The Chiefs have drafted more players from the Michigan State Spartans than from the Michigan Wolverines.

   a. True
   b. False

8. Which high-profile player acquired in a trade by the Chiefs from the New Orleans Saints franchise went on to be elected to the Hall of Fame?

a. Wide receiver Joe Horn

b. Cornerback Emmitt Thomas

c. Linebacker Willie Lanier

d. Offensive tackle Willie Roaf

9. Two teams from the NFL's Eastern Conference had future Hall-of-Fame quarterback Len Dawson before the Chiefs. Which two squads failed to maximize the considerable potential of Dawson?

   a. New York Giants and St. Louis Cardinals

   b. Philadelphia Eagles and Houston Oilers

   c. Pittsburgh Steelers and Cleveland Browns

   d. Baltimore Colts and Chicago Bears

10. In which city that shares its name with many males was Chiefs' franchise quarterback Patrick Mahomes born, in 1995?

    a. Tyler, Texas

    b. Eugene, Oregon

    c. Warren, Michigan

    d. Austin, Texas

11. Two players were teammates in college with the Georgia Bulldogs before taking the field together in Kansas City as well. Which two players were they?

    a. Defensive tackle Chris Jones and wide receiver Demarcus Robinson

    b. Running back Kareem Hunt and guard Parker Ehinger

    c. Cornerbacks Steven Nelson and Marcus Peters

d. Linebacker Ramik Wilson and wide receiver Chris Conley

12. Kansas City has never completed a trade with the Seattle Seahawks.

a. True
b. False

13. In 2009, the Chiefs traded star Tony Gonzalez to the Atlanta Falcons. What did they receive in return?

a. Two first-round draft picks and one third-round draft pick
b. Wide receiver Andre Rison and one third-round draft pick
c. One second-round draft pick
d. Tight end Tony Moeaki and one second-round draft pick

14. In 1983, the Chiefs drafted punter Jim Arnold, who played for Vanderbilt University, in the fifth round. What was his college team's nickname?

a. The Dust Devils
b. The Mastodons
c. The Commodores
d. The Fighting Camels

15. 63rd overall pick Travis Kelce played his college football as the tight end for which program before becoming a star with the Chiefs?

a. Cincinnati Bearcats
b. West Virginia Mountaineers

c. Washington Huskies

d. Florida Gators

16. In their entire history, the Chiefs have never traded away a player who was born in the state of Missouri.

a. True

b. False

17. Which prestigious Ivy League college program have the Chiefs dipped into during the NFL draft more often than any other?

a. Harvard University

b. Columbia University

c. Yale University

d. Princeton University

18. From which rival team did the Chiefs poach star safety Tyrann Mathieu as a free agent in 2019?

a. Arizona Cardinals

b. Philadelphia Eagles

c. Houston Texans

d. Indianapolis Colts

19. The talented and flamboyant Dante Hall was a member of which college squad before his time with the Chiefs?

a. Texas A&M Aggies

b. UCLA Bruins

c. Miami Hurricanes

d. Baylor Bears

20. Kansas City has completed more trades with the Detroit Lions than with any other NFL franchise.

    a. True
    b. False

QUIZ ANSWERS

1. A – Torrance, California

2. B – False

3. D – University of Notre Dame

4. C – Wide receiver Dwayne Bowe

5. A – Buffalo Bills

6. D – Crystal Lake University Sharks

7. B – False

8. D – Offensive tackle Willie Roaf

9. C – Pittsburgh Steelers and Cleveland Browns

10. A – Tyler, Texas

11. D – Linebacker Ramik Wilson and wide receiver Chris Conley

12. B – False

13. C – One second-round draft pick

14. C – The Commodores

15. A – Cincinnati Bearcats

16. B – False

17. D – Princeton University

18. C – Houston Texans

19. A – Texas A&M Aggies

20. B – False

DID YOU KNOW?

1. When the Chiefs needed to trade quarterback Alex Smith away from Kansas City in 2018 to make way for Patrick Mahomes, the franchise sent him to the Washington Football Team to get a third-round draft choice and cornerback Kendall Fuller, rather than simply cutting Smith.

2. In 1998, free-agent wide receiver Derrick Alexander decided to sign with Kansas City, partly to reunite with quarterback Elvis Grbac, who had thrown passes to Alexander when the two were college teammates with the Michigan Wolverines. It was a smart decision, as Alexander led the Chiefs in receiving yards that year.

3. The Chiefs and Denver Broncos have had a fairly heated rivalry throughout their existence, particularly during the 1990s. A few notable players not re-signed by Kansas City have signed directly with Denver to seek revenge, including defensive end Neil Smith, and running back Jamaal Charles.

4. Kansas City and the Baltimore Ravens have a rich history of player movement throughout the years. Significant names that have moved between the two teams include running back Priest Holmes, linebacker Terrell Suggs, quarterback Elvis Grbac, and wide receiver Sammy Watkins.

5. One of the worst free-agent signings made by the Chiefs occurred in 1998 when they gave running back Bam Morris a contract. Morris was ineffective with the team, but worse, he ended up receiving a 10-year prison sentence for a parole violation, putting an end to his NFL career.

6. In a decision that was very popular at the time, Kansas City signed defensive tackle Curley Culp, who had been drafted by the Denver Broncos but never played for them. Culp became a Pro Football Hall-of-Famer mostly due to his excellence while with the Chiefs.

7. One of the free agency decisions most regretted by Kansas City was allowing wide receiver Joe Horn to leave town to sign with the New Orleans Saints in 2000. Horn put up four seasons with 1000 yards receiving and over 50 touchdowns for the Saints, leaving a major hole in the Chiefs' offense.

8. Chiefs center Tim Grunhard played for one of the best college football teams ever, the 1988 Notre Dame Fighting Irish. The Irish not only went undefeated and won the National Championship that year but beat three previously unbeaten teams along the way.

9. Kansas City hit the jackpot when they selected linebacker Gary Spani in the 1978 NFL draft. Spani started for nine seasons, set a (then) NFL tackle record (157 in 1979), and was named 1983 NFL Man of the Year. They got all of this

from a hometown boy who was born in Kansas and went to school at Kansas State University.

10. There has always been animosity between the Chiefs and their division rival, the Denver Broncos. That animosity grew considerably in 2001 when Denver wide receiver Eddie Kennison requested his release from the team to retire. Denver granted this request and, less than a month later, Kennison signed with Kansas City, where he went on to play for seven more years.

CHAPTER 10:

IN THE DRAFT ROOM

QUIZ TIME!

1. The first Chiefs pick in the NFL's supplemental draft, guard Mark Adickes, attended Baylor University, where he played for the football team that went by which nickname?

    a. Lions
    b. Tigers
    c. Bears
    d. Wolves

2. For four consecutive years in the 1990s, the Chiefs traded out of the first round of the NFL draft, acquiring more proven talent in an effort to compete with the Buffalo Bills in the AFC.

    a. True
    b. False

3. From which of the following college football programs have the Chiefs drafted the most players?

a. Texas Longhorns
b. Texas Tech Red Raiders
c. Texas A&M Aggies
d. Texas-El Paso Miners

4. During the first round of the 2020 NFL draft, Kansas City congratulated which of the following players on becoming a Chief remotely, via webcam, because of the COVID-19 pandemic that prevented the usual handshakes on stage?

   a. Linebacker Willie Gay of the Mississippi State Bulldogs
   b. Wide receiver Mecole Hardman of the Georgia Bulldogs
   c. Running back Clyde Edwards-Helaire of the LSU Tigers
   d. Quarterback Patrick Mahomes of the Texas Tech Red Raiders

5. The Chiefs selected two teammates from the University of Mississippi Rebels 100 picks apart in the 2010 NFL draft. Which teammates did they choose with the 36th and 136th overall picks?

   a. Defensive back Javier Arenas and defensive end Cameron Sheffield
   b. Defensive end Tyson Jackson and kicker Ryan Succop
   c. Center Rodney Hudson and defensive tackle Jerrell Powe
   d. Wide receiver Dexter McCluster and defensive back Kendrick Lewis

6. How many times in history has Kansas City used a top-10 overall draft pick?

   a. 9 times
   b. 15 times
   c. 22 times
   d. 34 times

7. The Chiefs have never held the first overall pick in the NFL draft.

   a. True
   b. False

8. In 1962, the Chiefs drafted three players who never played any NFL games out of which school that is better known as a basketball powerhouse than a football school?

   a. Duke University
   b. University of North Carolina
   c. University of Kentucky
   d. Georgetown University

9. Quarterback Todd Blackledge was drafted by Kansas City seventh overall in the 1983 NFL entry draft. Which Hall of Fame quarterback was selected ahead of him that year?

   a. Jim Kelly of the Buffalo Bills
   b. Joe Montana of the San Francisco 49ers
   c. Dan Marino of the Miami Dolphins
   d. John Elway of the Denver Broncos

10. In the 1964 AFL draft, Kansas City selected not one but two quarterbacks. Who did they take to attempt to lock down the position?

   a. Pete Beathard in the 1st round and Roger Staubach in the 16th round
   b. Len Dawson in the 2nd round and Billy Moore in the 17th round
   c. Eddie Wilson in the 3rd round and Walt Rappold in the 26th round
   d. Mike Livingston in the 2nd round and Geoff Puddester in the 21st round

11. How high did Kansas City select defensive end Jared Allen in the 2004 NFL entry draft?

   a. 1st round, 6th overall
   b. 2nd round, 39th overall
   c. 4th round, 126th overall
   d. 7th round, 224th overall

12. Due in part to their longstanding rivalry with the Denver Broncos, Kansas City has never drafted a player from the University of Colorado.

   a. True
   b. False

13. How many draft choices did the Chiefs give up, to move up and select quarterback Patrick Mahomes in the 2017 NFL draft?

   a. 1
   b. 3

c. 4

d. 6

14. Linebacker Willie Lanier played four years of college ball for which program before being drafted by the Chiefs?

    a. Marshall University

    b. Grambling State University

    c. Morgan State University

    d. Pepperdine University

15. The Chiefs drafted two players from the Nebraska Cornhuskers who went on to play more than 180 NFL games each. Who were these players?

    a. Guard Will Shields and defensive end Neil Smith

    b. Running back Jerrel Wilson and defensive back Kevin Ross

    c. Linebacker Derrick Johnson and quarterback Alex Smith

    d. Tight end Jonathan Hayes and kicker Ryan Succop

16. Patrick Mahomes was such a talented athlete coming out of college that he was drafted in not one but three sports, basketball, baseball, and football.

    a. True

    b. False

17. Which team did the Chiefs trade up with so they could select future Hall-of-Fame tight end Tony Gonzalez in the first round of the NFL draft in 1997?

    a. Seattle Seahawks

    b. Oakland Raiders

c. Tampa Bay Buccaneers

d. Tennessee Oilers

18. Chiefs' cornerback Morris Claiborne has had a successful NFL career despite recording the lowest ever score on the Wonderlic test; an examination measuring cognitive ability on a 1-50 scale that is given to college students who may become NFL draft picks. What was Claiborne's score on the test?

a. 4 points

b. 9 points

c. 13 points

d. 17 points

19. Who did the Kansas City Chiefs select with their two first-round draft picks in 2008?

a. Defensive end Tyson Jackson and cornerback Brandon Flowers

b. Wide receiver Dwayne Bowe and defensive end Tamba Hali

c. Defensive tackle Glen Dorsey and guard Branden Albert

d. Safety Eric Berry and tight end Brad Cottam

20. Between 1990 and 2000, Kansas City enjoyed a stretch in which they selected at least one player per year who lasted 100 games in the NFL.

a. True

b. False

QUIZ ANSWERS

1. C – Bears

2. B – False

3. A – Texas Longhorns

4. C – Running back Clyde Edwards-Helaire of the LSU Tigers

5. D – Wide receiver Dexter McCluster and defensive back Kendrick Lewis

6. C – 22 times

7. B – False

8. A – Duke University

9. D – John Elway of the Denver Broncos

10. A – Pete Beathard in the 1st round and Roger Staubach in the 16th round

11. C – 4th round, 126th overall

12. B – False

13. B – 3

14. C – Morgan State University

15. A – Guard Will Shields and defensive end Neil Smith

16. B – False

17. D – Tennessee Oilers

18. A – 4 points

19. C – Defensive tackle Glen Dorsey and guard Branden Albert

20. B – False

DID YOU KNOW?

1. Defensive tackle Buck Buchanan, who was chosen 1st overall in 1963 out of Grambling State University, made history with the Chiefs as the first African American player ever taken first in the AFL draft. Buchanan went on to make the Pro Football Hall of Fame.

2. The most players Kansas City has drafted from any school is 16. This mark is held by the illustrious Notre Dame Fighting Irish. The school has not produced any Hall-of-Famers for the Chiefs, but center Tim Grunhard and linebacker Jim Lynch both played for a decade with the franchise.

3. Six times Kansas City has held the 23rd and 85th overall picks, making these their two most common landing spots in the NFL draft. The 85th position has not been very productive, but the Chiefs have landed useful players at 23rd overall, notably wide receiver Dwayne Bowe and linebacker Dee Ford.

4. Kansas City has made two LSU Tigers top five picks in the NFL draft, and they did it in back-to-back years, drafting teammates from the same position group. The team selected defensive tackle Glenn Dorsey 5th overall in 2008 and defensive end Tyson Jackson 3rd overall in 2009.

5. The Chiefs have a balanced draft history among their local schools, having taken 10 players from the University of

Kansas, 10 from the University of Missouri, and 6 from Kansas State University. The one that got away, though, hurt. Gale Sayers, the "Kansas Comet" was born in Kansas, played at the University of Kansas, and was drafted by the Kansas City Chiefs, who were in the AFL at the time. However, Sayers was also drafted by the NFL's Chicago Bears and decided to play there instead, becoming a legendary Hall-of-Famer in the process.

6. Kansas City has drafted precisely 13 players who have played a single game in the NFL. The most interesting was probably quarterback Dean Carlson, who spent two years mostly on the Chiefs' practice squad, was traded to Green Bay, and then signed with Kansas City again before seeing his only day of game action, finishing 7 for 15 with 116 passing yards.

7. In the 2007 NFL draft, Kansas City chose wide receiver Dwayne Bowe 23rd overall out of Louisiana State University. Fellow LSU wideout Craig Davis and quarterback Jamarcus Russell were also selected in the first round, marking the first time in NFL history that a school's quarterback and his top two targets had all been drafted in Round One.

8. The smallest draft classes ever selected by the Chiefs in the NFL entry draft came in 1993 and 2002 when they took just five players each year. 1993's draft class worked out better, as Kansas City's new guard, Will Shields, went on to make the Pro Football Hall of Fame.

9. In 2008, the Chiefs drafted three different players named Brandon. All three had successful NFL careers, as guard Branden Albert, and cornerbacks Brandon Flowers and Brandon Carr all played over 100 professional games.

10. The latest pick the Chiefs have made in the NFL draft was running back Pat McNeil from the Baylor Bears, whom the team chose 472nd overall in 1976. McNeil beat the odds and suited up for 13 NFL games, rushing for 26 yards and adding 33 receiving yards.

CHAPTER 11:

COACHES, GMS, & OWNERS

QUIZ TIME!

1. Who serves as the Chiefs' first general manager?

    a. Brett Veach

    b. Andy Reid

    c. Mike Borgonzi

    d. Britt Reid

2. Kansas City general manager Carl Peterson once proposed a deal to the New England Patriots that would have sent Chiefs' icon Priest Holmes to Massachusetts in exchange for a young and then little-known Tom Brady.

    a. True

    b. False

3. The Chiefs' first head coach, Hank Stram, lasted for how long in that position with the franchise?

    a. 8 games

    b. 2 seasons

    c. 6 seasons

    d. 15 seasons

4. The Chiefs' most recent coach, Andy Reid, rose through the coaching ranks in the NCAA, starting his coaching career with which program?

   a. Brigham Young University
   b. San Francisco State University
   c. University of Texas-El Paso
   d. University of Missouri

5. Who has owned the Kansas City Chiefs for the longest amount of time?

   a. Clark Hunt
   b. Scott Pioli
   c. Lamar Hunt
   d. Brett Veach

6. Of all the Kansas City bench bosses who have coached over 40 NFL games with the team, which one had the lowest winning percentage at only .313?

   a. Marv Levy
   b. Todd Haley
   c. John Mackovic
   d. Herman Edwards

7. Kansas City is the only NFL franchise to have a player rise from competing on the field for the team to ownership of the team.

   a. True
   b. False

8. Which coach led the Chiefs to their first NFL championship?

a. Hank Stram

b. Marty Schottenheimer

c. Andy Reid

d. Dick Vermeil

9. Which Kansas City general manager once took the field as a player on the Green Bay Packers before getting the chance to guide the Chiefs from the front office?

a. Scott Pioli

b. Brett Veach

c. John Dorsey

d. Carl Peterson

10. Who is the Kansas City leader in coaching wins?

a. Hank Stram

b. Marty Schottenheimer

c. Dick Vermeil

d. Andy Reid

11. The shortest ownership term for a Kansas City Chiefs owner is held by Clark Hunt. For how long did he own the team?

a. 8 months

b. 3 years

c. 7 years

d. 15 years

12. Coach Andy Reid's 2020 season is the benchmark in terms of winning percentage, as he led the team to a .875 winning percentage in the regular season.

a. True

b. False

13. How many of the Chiefs' thirteen head coaches have spent their entire NFL coaching career with Kansas City?

    a. 1
    b. 3
    c. 6
    d. 10

14. Which Chiefs general manager has led the franchise to the most playoff appearances?

    a. Jack Steadman
    b. Jim Schaaf
    c. Carl Peterson
    d. Brett Veach

15. In 10 seasons coaching the Chiefs, how many times did coach Marty Schottenheimer finish above .500?

    a. 4
    b. 5
    c. 9
    d. 10

16. At one point in their history, the Chiefs employed four coaches over a decade who had all started for Kansas City at some point during their playing careers.

    a. True
    b. False

17. How did Clark Hunt become the majority owner of the Kansas City Chiefs in 2006?

    a. He purchased the team when the previous owners wished to sell.
    b. He inherited the team from his father.
    c. He forced a takeover of the corporation that had previously owned the team.
    d. He was hired as CEO of the company that owned the team.

18. How many head coaches have roamed the sidelines for the Chiefs in their history?

    a. 7
    b. 10
    c. 13
    d. 17

19. The Associated Press has named how many Chiefs coaches as the league's top coach?

    a. 0
    b. 3
    c. 5
    d. 6

20. Chiefs' owner Lamar Hunt once proposed trading franchises with New York Yankees owner George Steinbrenner, as part of a business deal.

    a. True
    b. False

QUIZ ANSWERS

1. C – Mike Borgonzi

2. B – False

3. D – 15 seasons

4. A – Brigham Young University

5. C – Lamar Hunt

6. D – Herman Edwards

7. B – False

8. A – Hank Stram

9. C – John Dorsey

10. B – Marty Schottenheimer

11. D – 15 years

12. A – True

13. C –6

14. C – Carl Peterson

15. C – 9

16. B – False

17. B – He inherited the team from his father.

18. C – 13

19. A – 0

20. B – False

DID YOU KNOW?

1. Only twice in team history have the Chiefs fired a coach midway through a season. The first time occurred in 1977 when Paul Wiggin was let go and Tom Bettis took over just for the remainder of the year. Then, in 2011, Todd Haley got fired and Romeo Crennel took his place, with Crennel lasting through the 2012 season.

2. Not a single person has served as both coach and general manager of the Chiefs. In many organizations, this power structure has become common, but in Kansas City there has always been a clear and distinct hierarchy for the men running the show.

3. Chiefs general manager Jim Schaaf spent six years as an executive for Major League Baseball's Kansas City Athletics from 1961 through 1966 before switching sports, but staying in the same town, to work with the Chiefs instead.

4. Chiefs head coach Herm Edwards eventually wrote a book named after one of his most famous press conference quotes. The book was titled "You Play to Win the Game

5. The Chiefs' original general manager, Don Rossi, lasted only part of a season with the franchise and did not make it from Dallas to Kansas City with the team's move. Instead, Rossi turned his attention to the links, where became president of the National Golf Foundation and

executive director of the Golf Course Builders Association of America.

6. For eight years after his tenure as general manager of the Chiefs was over, Carl Peterson was the chairman of USA Football, a governing body dedicated to growing the sport of football among the youth of America. When Peterson stepped down, he was succeeded in this position by four-star Army general Ray Odierno.

7. In 2008, the 54th birthday of Chiefs head coach Herman Edwards, April 27, fell on the day of the NFL draft. As a gift, general manager Carl Peterson let Edwards choose the team's 140th overall pick. Edwards exclaimed "I want Brandon Carr!" and the team indeed chose cornerback Carr, who played for four years with Kansas City.

8. Chiefs head coach Andy Reid was always a larger-than-life figure. At the age of 13, Reid participated in a youth Punt, Pass, and Kick competition where he towered over the other kids because he was 6'1" and 207 pounds at the time. Occasionally, video of this event is shown during Kansas City broadcasts to entertain viewers.

9. Although he was known as a "player's coach," Chiefs bench boss Dick Vermeil was not above using the media to motivate his players. At one point in 2004, Vermeil lit into young running back Larry Johnson, stating that Johnson needed to "take the diaper off and go play."

10. Never in league history has a Kansas City general manager been awarded the *Sporting News* NFL Executive

of the Year Award. Scott Pioli received the honor twice, back-to-back in 2003 and 2004, but he was with the New England Patriots at the time and did not move to Kansas City until 2009.

CHAPTER 12:

ODDS & ENDS

QUIZ TIME!

1. Which Chief has won the most league MVP trophies while playing for Kansas City?

   a. Quarterback Len Dawson

   b. Running back Priest Holmes

   c. Linebacker Derrick Thomas

   d. Quarterback Patrick Mahomes

2. The first Chief to win any major award given out by the NFL was franchise tight end Tony Gonzalez.

   a. True

   b. False

3. For which season did the Chiefs win their first Vince Lombardi Trophy as Super Bowl Champions?

   a. 1966

   b. 1969

   c. 1975

   d. 1982

4. In 2019, the NFL announced its 100th-Anniversary All-Time Team, recognizing the 100 greatest players from the first 100 years of NFL history. How many of these players suited up for the Chiefs?

    a. 3 on offense, 3 on defense, and 1 on special teams
    b. 4 on offense, 6 on defense, and 2 on special teams
    c. 2 on offense, 5 on defense, and 0 on special teams
    d. 7 on offense, 4 on defense, and 1 on special teams

5. Between 2015 and 2019, the Chiefs put up the best record against divisional opponents of any NFL team in history during any five-year stretch. What was their win/loss record against the Broncos, Raiders, and Chargers during this time?

    a. 21-9
    b. 24-6
    c. 27-3
    d. 29-1

6. What is Mitch Holthus's connection to the Kansas City Chiefs?

    a. An architect who designed and built Arrowhead Stadium for Chiefs owner Lamar Hunt
    b. A beloved groundskeeper who has worked for the Chiefs since 1977
    c. A player agent who represented Christian Okoye, Tamba Hali, and several others
    d. A longtime radio announcer for the Chiefs on their home station

7. The Kansas City Chiefs have the most wins of any franchise in NFL history.

   a. True
   b. False

8. Heisman Trophy-winning quarterback Eric Crouch converted to safety with the Chiefs after excelling under center for which college program?

   a. Nebraska Cornhuskers
   b. Alabama Crimson Tide
   c. Notre Dame Fighting Irish
   d. Florida State Seminoles

9. Although his average yards per punt was 44.8, Chiefs' punter Dustin Colquitt set the Kansas City record for longest punt in franchise history with one that traveled how far?

   a. 62 yards
   b. 69 yards
   c. 73 yards
   d. 81 yards

10. Which Chiefs kicker, with at least 50 kicks attempted, holds the team's highest field goal percentage, at 90.3% made?

   a. Cairo Santos
   b. Nick Lowery
   c. Harrison Butker
   d. Jan Stenerud

11. Linebacker Terrell Suggs was a key veteran presence on a championship team in Kansas City and he also won an NFL championship with which other franchise?

    a. Arizona Cardinals
    b. New York Giants
    c. Dallas Cowboys
    d. Baltimore Ravens

12. Kansas City was the first NFL team to win the Super Bowl after losing the previous year.

    a. True
    b. False

13. What is the most points the Chiefs have scored in any Super Bowl?

    a. 31 points
    b. 38 points
    c. 44 points
    d. 52 points

14. Of the Chiefs in the Pro Football Hall of Fame, safety Johnny Robinson was the first to play with the franchise. What year did he begin playing with the team?

    a. 1968
    b. 1965
    c. 1962
    d. 1960

15. Two Chiefs, kickers Nick Lowery and Harrison Butker, share the franchise record for the longest field goal made. How long were these record-setting kicks?

    a. 51 yards
    b. 56 yards
    c. 58 yards
    d. 62 yards

16. Hall-of-Fame Chiefs kicker Jan Stenerud has *missed* more field goals during his Chiefs career than any other Kansas City player has even *attempted*.

    a. True
    b. False

17. Who was the Chiefs' first Super Bowl MVP?

    a. Quarterback Len Dawson
    b. Linebacker Willie Lanier
    c. Tight end Travis Kelce
    d. Quarterback Patrick Mahomes

18. Which opposing team have the Chiefs never faced in the Super Bowl?

    a. Tampa Bay Buccaneers
    b. Dallas Cowboys
    c. San Francisco 49ers
    d. Minnesota Vikings

19. In which state have the Chiefs competed in the most Super Bowls?

a. Arizona

b. California

c. Florida

d. Louisiana

20. The Chiefs are undefeated in Super Bowl games that were held in outdoor stadiums.

a. True

b. False

QUIZ ANSWERS

1. D – Quarterback Patrick Mahomes

2. B – False

3. B – 1969

4. A – 3 on offense, 3 on defense, and 1 on special teams

5. C – 27-3

6. D – A longtime radio announcer for the Chiefs on their home station

7. B – False

8. A – Nebraska Cornhuskers

9. D – 81 yards

10. C – Harrison Butker

11. D – Baltimore Ravens

12. B – False

13. A – 31 points

14. D – 1960

15. C – 58 yards

16. B – False

17. A – Quarterback Len Dawson

18. B – Dallas Cowboys

19. C – Florida

20. B – False

DID YOU KNOW?

1. Five Chiefs have won the NFL's Walter Payton Man of the Year Award. This is tied for the most of any franchise with Payton's former team, the Chicago Bears.

2. The only time the Walter Payton Man of the Year Award has been given to the same franchise in back-to-back years, it was given to two Kansas City Chiefs. Linebacker Willie Lanier was the recipient in 1972 and quarterback Len Dawson won the award in 1973.

3. Chiefs icon Jan Stenerud was the first NFL player ever born in Norway. Stenerud was a model of consistency for over a decade with the Chiefs, hitting 97% of his extra-point attempts, and is one of just three players who were exclusively kickers to be elected to the Pro Football Hall of Fame.

4. Kansas City has been shut out when it comes to the NFL's Offensive Rookie of the Year Award. No Chief has ever been selected since the award was created in 1967.

5. Four Chiefs have won the NFL's Defensive Rookie of the Year Award. Defensive tackle Bill Maas was the first, in 1984. Legendary linebacker Derrick Thomas came next, in 1989. And two cornerbacks, Dale Carter in 1992 and Marcus Peters in 2015, round out the recipients.

6. The Chiefs have both a female cheerleading squad (with the rather obvious name Kansas City Chiefs Cheerleaders)

and a male drumline (called Chiefs Rumble) that help support the team at games and make various appearances in the local community.

7. The Chiefs' value is estimated at $2.3 billion by Forbes magazine, which ranks them as the 23rd most valuable NFL team, right between the Carolina Panthers and New Orleans Saints.

8. The Chiefs mascot has undergone several changes over the years. At first, it was a horse named Warpaint, ridden by a man in a ceremonial headdress, that would circle the field after touchdowns. In 1989, the team switched to a person in a wolf costume, known as K.C. Wolf and named after a group of fans dubbed The Wolfpack. In 2009, Kansas City brought back Warpaint (though it was a new horse) and gave him a female rider instead.

9. In 2020, the Chiefs tied with three other teams (Green Bay Packers, Baltimore Ravens, and Seattle Seahawks) for the league lead by seeing seven of their players get invited to the NFL's Pro Bowl.

10. Since September 29th, 2014, Chiefs fans have held the Guinness World Record for the loudest outdoor stadium. They claimed the record at Arrowhead Stadium during a Monday Night Football game versus the New England Patriots, reaching 142.2 decibels to best the Seattle Seahawks' old record of 137.6 decibels at CenturyLink Field.

CONCLUSION

There you have it, an amazing collection of Chiefs trivia, information, and statistics at your fingertips!

Regardless of how you fared on the quizzes, we hope that you found this book entertaining, enlightening, and educational. Ideally, you knew many of these details but also learned more about the history of the Kansas City Chiefs, their players, coaches, management, and some of the quirky stories surrounding the team.

If you got a little peek into the colorful details that make being a fan so much more enjoyable, then mission accomplished!

The good news is that the trivia doesn't have to stop there! Spread the word. Challenge your fellow Chiefs fans to see if they can do any better. Share some of the stories with the next generation to help them become Kansas City supporters too.

If you are a big enough Chiefs fan, consider creating your own quiz with some of the details you know that weren't presented here, and then test your friends to see if they can match your knowledge.

The Kansas City Chiefs are a storied franchise. They have a long history with multiple periods of success, and a few that were less than successful. They've had glorious superstars, iconic moments, hilarious tales, but most of all they have wonderful, passionate fans. Thank you for being one of them.

Manufactured by Amazon.ca
Bolton, ON